SHE CAUGHT THE LIGHT

Williamina Stevens Fleming: Astronomer

Written by **Kathryn Lasky**   Illustrated by **Julianna Swaney**

HARPER
An Imprint of HarperCollinsPublishers

T0033476

More than one hundred years ago in the city of Dundee, Scotland, a very smart baby girl was born. Her name was Williamina. They called her Mina.

Her father was a carver and a gilder. He carved picture frames and gilded them in gold leaf. But he also had a hobby—making photographs.

He and his wife knew their baby was bright because she was so curious.

Even when she was very little, she loved watching her father polish the sheets of silver plate with special chemicals to catch the light for his photographs.

Mina would follow her father into his darkroom to see the magic as the faces of a family portrait emerged on the plates, melting out of the darkness like stars in the night.

And Mina had as many questions as there were stars in the sky.

Why do the chemicals work?

How does the light get onto the plate?

Can I do this someday?

When Mina was seven years old her father died. Her mother and her brothers tried to keep the shop going but failed. Everyone had to go to work, including Mina when she became a bit older. So when she was just fourteen she began teaching school.

When Williamina was twenty, she married James Fleming. They sailed from Dundee to Boston, and then—shockingly—he disappeared.

Mina was left all alone and friendless in a strange city. Or almost alone, for she soon discovered she was expecting a baby.

Williamina had to find a job. Fast. On top of one of the highest hills in the city of Cambridge, Massachusetts, there was a building with a big dome, an observatory. It was the Harvard College Observatory for studying the stars. Professor Pickering was the director and lived in the connecting house with his wife, Elizabeth. Williamina became their maid.

She dusted. She swept. She scrubbed. And she asked many questions.

Elizabeth and Edward Pickering sensed that Williamina was smart.

One day the professor was complaining to his male assistants about their astronomical calculations. The assistants' job was to study the spectra, or the rainbows of colors of starlight, recorded by the telescope's spectroscope.

But the assistants were making mistakes. The professor was upset.

"My Scottish maid could do better!" he thundered at them.

Mrs. Pickering overheard this and thought, *Yes! Why not?*

She urged her husband to give Mina a chance.

Mina had learned a lot just by being in the presence of Professor Pickering, although she was his housekeeper and not his student. She knew he was exploring not only where the stars were in the sky but what the stars were made of. She knew that the elements in stars—carbon, oxygen, nitrogen—were the very same ones that make up the Earth and even the human beings on Earth. The hidden, the unknown, and the unseen fascinated Williamina. This was the secret language of starlight. Mina was excited.

She learned that when the light of stars passed through the prism of the spectroscope, it blossomed into rainbows of colors. Glass plates recorded this spectrum, but not in color. There was no such thing as color photography back then.

On the plate, the rainbow of each star's colors was filled with dark vertical lines. These lines made a pattern that was the key to the mysteries of the stars. By studying the lines, the secrets of a star's light were revealed—the chemical elements that made up the star itself.

For example, the lines that indicate hydrogen were in the red, blue, and violet parts of the spectrum. From star to star the rainbow varied because each star was made up of slightly different elements. As the whorls of lines on a human being's fingers differ from person to person, these vertical lines became the fingerprints of the stars.

It was as if each star had a different personality, and this was what puzzled and excited Mina the most. The differences. The lines indicating the elements within the band were like fingerprints across the glass plates. Mina wanted to sort them out like puzzle pieces—these little pieces of heaven's puzzle. She began to classify them into an order that would show how one star differed from another.

To capture the light of these stars, you needed to use a telescope. But the most unfair thing was that Williamina and, later, other women astronomers were never allowed to look through a telescope for "health reasons." Women, the men said, were too fragile. In the unheated observatory dome, they might catch cold!

So what the women saw were the glass plates that recorded the spectra. The plates were removed from the telescope's spectrograph and like film were put in a chemical bath to develop. Gradually the lines would appear. It reminded Mina of the magic that transpired in her father's darkroom back in Dundee, Scotland.

Williamina was becoming very good at sorting out all these lines, but each day her belly grew larger with her baby. Williamina was exhausted.

She decided to go back to Scotland to give birth and get help from her mother. So she set sail. Once home, she gave birth to her baby, a boy whom she named Edward.

But the stars called to Mina even as she rocked her baby, far away in Dundee. And like ghostly charms in the night, the rainbows of starlight floated through her dreams. She had to return to Boston.

By the time she returned, Professor Pickering was so impressed with Mina's talents that he had begun to hire more women to compute the light of stars.

But it was not always the secrets of starlight that she found on those glass plates. One day Williamina was peering at a plate and saw something very intriguing. She described it as a swirling cloud of gases buried in the constellation of Orion. The light from this mysterious object had to have traveled over one thousand years to reach Earth. The location within the Orion constellation was known to be a stellar nursery—a place where stars are born. The cloud of gases she saw resembled a horse's head. It reared up, blocking the stars behind it.

No one had seen this before, and Mina's discovery became known as the Horsehead Nebula. It was important because it would give astronomers clues about how stars are born and about the composition of our own home galaxy, the Milky Way.

Mina knew that this was a significant discovery. But more discoveries would follow, and more women came to the observatory. These women became known as the human computers.

They were paid twenty-five cents an hour. The men were paid many times more. It was unfair. Mina complained to Professor Pickering.

Mina wondered if he ever thought about how she had a home of her own to keep and a child to raise. She helped her son, Edward, with his homework every night. Put bandages on his skinned knees. Played board games with him. Made fudge. And on top of all these motherly tasks, she decoded the light of the stars and the secrets of the universe.

Williamina was not simply catching the light and sorting the stars above the Harvard Observatory but also decoding the glass plates sent to her from another observatory in Peru. There were new starry treasures to be discovered in the southern hemisphere—stars like the "Demon star," Algol. Algol was called a winking star, as its brightness often changed. Williamina made a small pair of dolls in honor of Algol's winking. One of the dolls was dressed in bright clothes; the other was dressed in darker ones.

Making dolls based on stars was Mina's hobby. She gave them to children's hospitals.

But most of her time was spent sorting and classifying the stars and cracking the secret code of their light.

Her father back in Dundee had created portraits of families. Now she was creating a portrait of the universe that astronomers would use for over a century.

In 1898, Williamina was appointed curator of astronomical photographs.
She was the first woman to be given an official title at Harvard University.

Williamina Fleming believed that the universe, with its billions of stars, was a riddle. It was a mystery waiting to be solved. She captured the light to help solve that riddle. And by the end of her life she had classified over 10,000 stars.

TIMELINE

1857: Williamina Paton Stevens is born in Dundee, Scotland, on May 15.

1877: She marries James Orr Fleming.

1879: She becomes a maid in the home of Edward Pickering, the director of the Harvard College Observatory, and his wife, Elizabeth Pickering, in Cambridge, Massachusetts.

1881: Pickering adds Williamina to the observatory's permanent staff.

1888: Williamina discovers the Horsehead Nebula.

1890: For the first edition of the *Draper Catalogue of Stellar Spectra*, Williamina classifies 28,266 spectra of 10,351 stars on 633 plates—by far the most extensive star compilation of the era.

1893: She attends the Chicago Congress of Astronomy and Physics. In her remarks she speaks out for women's equality and the rightful place of women in the field of astronomy.

1898: Williamina is nominated for the Bruce Medal of Astronomy.

1899: Williamina is appointed curator of astronomical photographs and becomes the first woman to have an official title at Harvard University.

1900: She accompanies the Harvard expedition to Washington, Georgia, to observe a solar eclipse.

1906: Williamina becomes the first American woman elected to honorary membership in England's Royal Astronomical Society.

1911: Williamina Fleming dies on May 21 in Boston at the age of fifty-four.

GLOSSARY

Daguerreotype: An early photographic process using plates made of silver or copper coated with special chemicals that react to light.

Dwarf star: A small star with low luminosity that burns hydrogen at a slow rate in comparison to giant stars. Our sun is a dwarf star.

Element: A substance composed of atoms that cannot be broken down into a simpler substance by chemical means.

Galaxy: A large collection of stars with gases and dust that is held together by gravity. Our own galaxy is called the Milky Way.

Giant star: A very large, bright star that burns hydrogen at a much faster rate than a dwarf star does. Giant stars have much shorter life spans than the slower-burning dwarf stars.

Light-year: The distance that light travels over a period of one year, about 5.88 trillion miles.

Magellanic clouds: Two irregular galaxies that appear like dusty lanes in the sky in the Southern Hemisphere and orbit our Milky Way galaxy.

Nebula: A cloud of gas and dust in interstellar space.

Nova: The sudden appearance of a bright and seemingly new star, seen as a flare-up that over weeks or months slowly fades.

Prism: A wedge- or rectangular-shaped piece of glass designed to separate white light into colors.

Spectroscope: A device with prisms attached to the light-collecting end of a telescope. By separating the light into colors, the prisms enable scientists to analyze what elements are in a star they are observing.

Spectrum: A rainbow of colors produced when light passes through a prism.

Stellar nursery: A region in outer space where stars are born.

Supergiant: A very large star, bigger than a giant star.

Variable star: A star whose brightness changes with time.

BIOGRAPHY

Williamina Paton Stevens Fleming was born May 15, 1857, in Dundee, Scotland. She was what we would now call self-educated. She held no degree from any institution of higher learning, and yet she was the first woman to be appointed to a titled position at Harvard University: the curator of astronomical photographs. In her lifetime she analyzed and classified the spectra of over 10,000 stars. And most important, she devised the classification system that helped map the universe for future astronomers. One of her most famous discoveries was the Horsehead Nebula. She worked at the Harvard College Observatory from 1879 until her death on May 21, 1911. She was the first member of what was called Harvard's "human computers": more than a dozen women who analyzed the spectra of the stars. Williamina Fleming in her lifetime of studying the glass plates discovered ten novae and three hundred variable stars. Sixty years after her death, a lunar crater was named for her.

AUTHOR'S NOTE

I read that every atom in our body comes from a star. We are, in short, star stuff. I live in Cambridge, Massachusetts, exactly three quarters of a mile from the Harvard College Observatory. When I discovered that in the late nineteenth century there was a team of women at the observatory known as the "human computers," I was intrigued. Harvard had never been welcoming to women. Indeed, the president of Harvard at that time was shocked by the idea of young women attending the university. It was not until 1963 that women were granted degrees from Harvard.

And yet it was these women, the human computers, who mapped the stars. The greatest irony was that they were not even permitted to look through telescopes, for they were thought too fragile to withstand the cold winter nights. So it was

only men who were allowed the live view through the spectroscope to witness the actual colors of the stars, the individual rainbows that ranged from reddish at one end through orange, yellow, green, and then blue to indigo to violet at the other end. Because there was no color photography, the rainbow was shown on the plates as intervals of gray shadows interspersed with black lines. And that was what the women saw and decoded to discover the elements of the stars.

These women ultimately laid the groundwork for twentieth-century astronomy. Working alongside Williamina Fleming on the stellar classification system was Henrietta Swan Leavitt, who discovered the luminosity relationship for certain variable stars. Her calculations became the basis for Edwin Hubble's estimations about the distances to the stars. Also on the team were Antonia Maury, who researched stellar spectra of supergiants and dwarf stars, and Annie Jump Cannon, who refined the classification system. The woman who helped to make the

classification process possible was Mary Anna Palmer Draper, who donated tens of thousands of dollars for the *Draper Catalogue of Stellar Spectra*.

I just knew I had to tell their story, but I decided to focus on Williamina. To travel across the ocean from Scotland, then to be abandoned by her husband and raise a child on her own in a foreign country—what a poignant story!

Science proceeds by trial and error. At the time that Williamina Fleming was working, she thought she was classifying stars by the amount of hydrogen each star contained. The resulting scheme is still in use, and for more than a century it has been an invaluable tool for organizing stellar information. But shortly after quantum theory was developed in 1915, scientists realized that the appearance of lines in the spectrum is actually due mainly to a star's temperature and not its composition. Nevertheless, Fleming's classification was vitally important, and it enabled the modern science of astronomy. Isaac Newton once said, "If I have seen further than others, it is by standing on the shoulders of giants." Williamina was one of those giants for twentieth- and twenty-first-century astronomers. She was in my mind a hero of the stars. And I was starstruck!

BIBLIOGRAPHY

Burleigh, Robert. *Look Up! Henrietta Leavitt, Pioneering Woman Astronomer.* Illus. Raúl Colón. New York: Simon & Schuster/Paula Wiseman Books, 2013.

Gerber, Carole. *Annie Jump Cannon, Astronomer.* Illus. Christina Wald. Gretna, LA: Pelican Publishing, 2011.

Haley, Paul A., "Williamina Fleming and the Harvard College Observatory," *Antiquarian Astronomer*, no. 11 (June 2017), 2–32.

Hirshfeld, Alan, "Williamina Fleming: Brief Life of a Spectrographic Pioneer: 1857–1911," *Harvard Magazine*, January–February 2017, 48–49.

Hoffleit, E. Dorrit. "Pioneering Women in the Spectral Classification of Stars," *Physics in Perspective*, vol. 4, no. 4 (December 2002), 370–398.

James, C. Renée, "Edward and Mina," *Astronomy*, vol. 30, no. 7 (July 2002), 46–50.

Sobel, Dava. *The Glass Universe: How the Ladies of the Harvard Observatory Took the Measure of the Stars.* New York: Viking, 2016.

Van Dyke, Joyce. *The Women Who Mapped the Stars*, a play presented by the Central Square Theater, Cambridge, MA, 2018.